What's it like to be a...
FOREST RANGER

Written by Michael J. Pellowski
Illustrated by George Ulrich

Troll Associates

Special Consultant: Robert Conklin, *U.S. Forest Ranger, New York State.*

Library of Congress Cataloging-in-Publication Data

Pellowski, Michael.
   Forest ranger / by Michael J. Pellowski; illustrated by George
Ulrich.
     p.   cm.—(What's it like to be a...)
   Summary: Outlines the various jobs performed by forest rangers,
including firefighting, inspecting trees for disease and insect
damage, and keeping track of animals and the water supply.
   ISBN 0-8167-1422-3 (lib. bdg.)   ISBN 0-8167-1423-1 (pbk.)
   1. Forest rangers—Vocational guidance—Juvenile literature.
[1. Forest rangers. 2. Occupations.] I. Ulrich, George, ill.
II. Title. III. Series.
SD387.F6P45 1989
634.9—dc19   88-10355

What's it like to be a...
FOREST RANGER

Fire Tower

A thin stream of smoke is rising from above
the trees. Woods are burning!

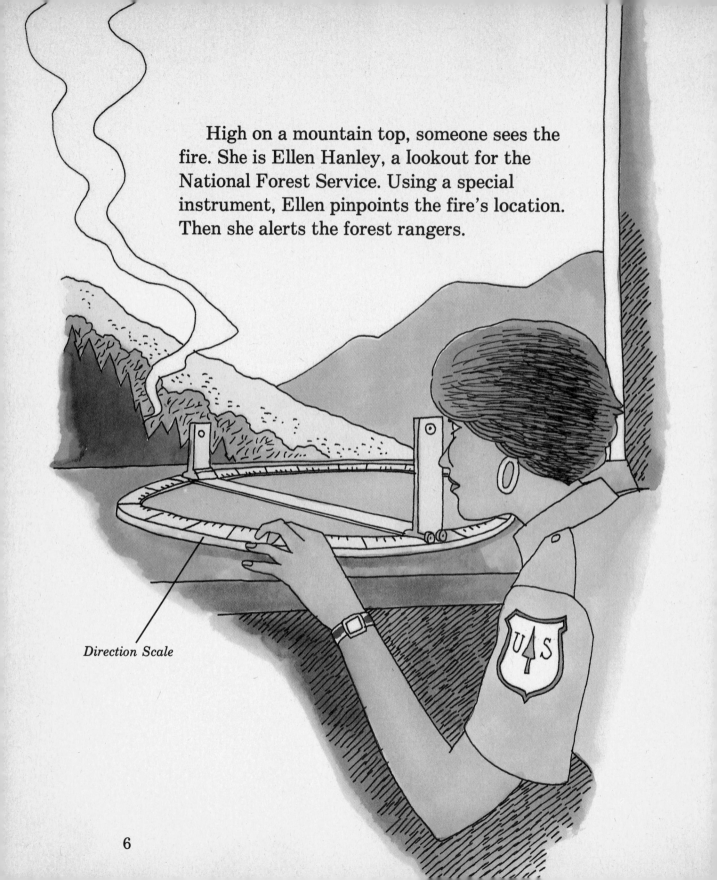

High on a mountain top, someone sees the fire. She is Ellen Hanley, a lookout for the National Forest Service. Using a special instrument, Ellen pinpoints the fire's location. Then she alerts the forest rangers.

Direction Scale

NATIONAL FOREST

Microphone

"Hanley to ground crew! Hanley to ground crew!" she calls into her two-way radio. "Fire burning! Fire burning!"

Jim Dayton, the head ranger, answers the call. He marks the fire's location on a map. Then he sends the fire-fighting crew into action.

Spade

Portable Fire Extinguisher

Pickup Truck

Hard Hat

Ax

The fire—started by some dry leaves, twigs, and grass—is spreading fast. The ranger yells to the crew chief, "Let's make a firebreak, before this fire starts climbing up the trees!"

A firebreak is a special way to fight a forest fire. The rangers form a line. They go to work, removing anything that might burn. They use shovels, chain saws, and other hand tools. When the fire reaches the firebreak, it cannot spread any further.

Hose Gun

Portable Fire Extinguisher

Mattock

Spade

Safety Goggles

Firebreak

Chain Saw

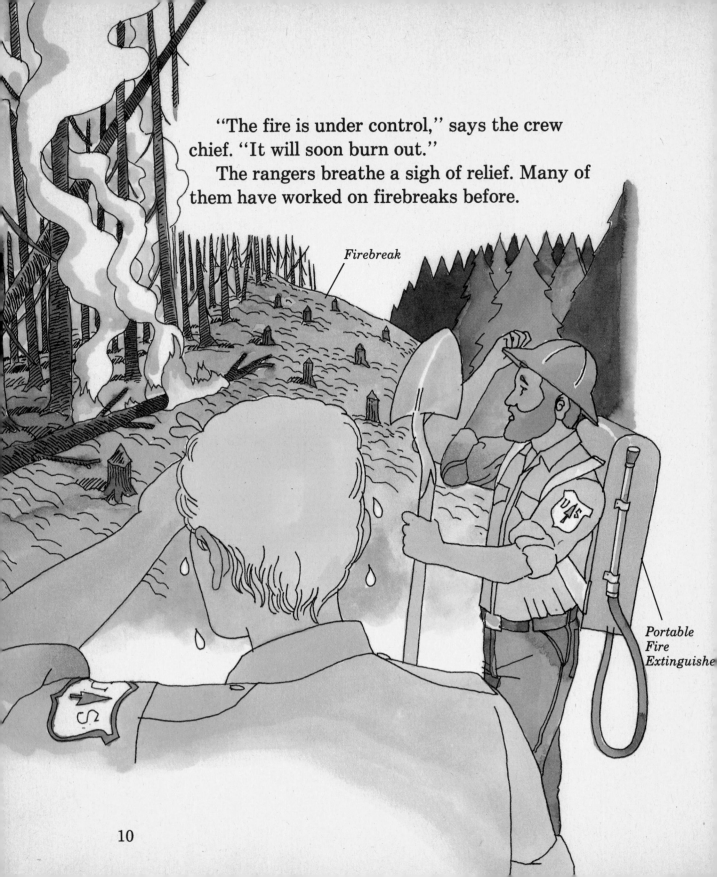

"The fire is under control," says the crew chief. "It will soon burn out."

The rangers breathe a sigh of relief. Many of them have worked on firebreaks before.

Firebreak

Portable Fire Extinguishe

Smoke Jumper

Helicopter

Seaplane Dropping
Water

150-Gallon
Water Bucket

Diesel
Engine

Safety
Roll Bar

Diesel
Fuel Tank

Blade

Hydraulic
Jack

Crawler Tracks

Bulldozer

For big fires, rangers use bulldozers to make firebreaks. They also use airplanes and helicopters to reach fires that are burning out of control. Special fire fighters parachute down to fires that ground crews cannot reach. They are called "smoke jumpers."

Cab

Fuel Tank

Side
Rails

Mud Flap

Brake Lights

After the fire is out, the crew returns to the
ranger station.

"Good work, Ellen," says Jim Dayton to the
lookout.

"Thanks," Ellen replies.

Ellen introduces the rangers to a camper named Bob.

"Bob's been watching," Ellen says. "He wants to be a ranger someday."

"I want to fight forest fires, just like you," Bob says to the rangers.

The head ranger smiles.
"Forest rangers do a lot more than fight fires," he says. "Each ranger has special training to do many jobs."

"Will you tell me all about forest rangers?"
Bob asks.

"Sure," says Jim. "Let's go into the ranger
station."

"All rangers must go to college to learn about forestry," Jim begins. "Then they are trained in one of many fields."

The head ranger pauses.
"Do you like the outdoors?" he asks Bob.
"You bet!"
"Well, that's a good start," says Jim.
"Rangers love the outdoors!"

Bedroll

Back Pack

Some rangers specialize in tree diseases and insect control. They inspect forests for signs of trouble. It's their job to make sure the trees stay healthy.

Back Pack

18

Sometimes, a ranger may spot bark beetles in the trees. These insects eat through the tree bark and cause disease. Trees with bark beetles have to be sprayed.

Bark Beetle

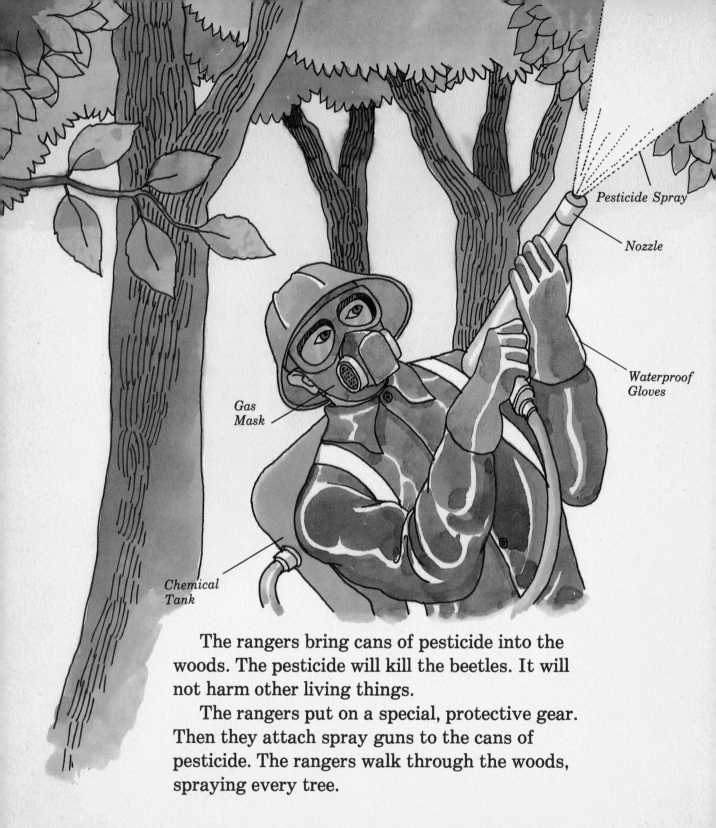

Pesticide Spray

Nozzle

Waterproof
Gloves

Gas
Mask

Chemical
Tank

The rangers bring cans of pesticide into the
woods. The pesticide will kill the beetles. It will
not harm other living things.

The rangers put on a special, protective gear.
Then they attach spray guns to the cans of
pesticide. The rangers walk through the woods,
spraying every tree.

Healthy trees are often used for lumber. These trees are called timber. Timber control is the job of other rangers. Timber control means that some trees must be cut down to allow other trees to grow.

Timber

Spare Tire

Four-Wheel Drive Jeep

Spade

Extra Fuel Tank

Map

21

Rangers decide which trees to cut. They measure the trees to see how much lumber there will be. Then the trees to be cut are marked with white paint.

Spray Paint

Tape Measure

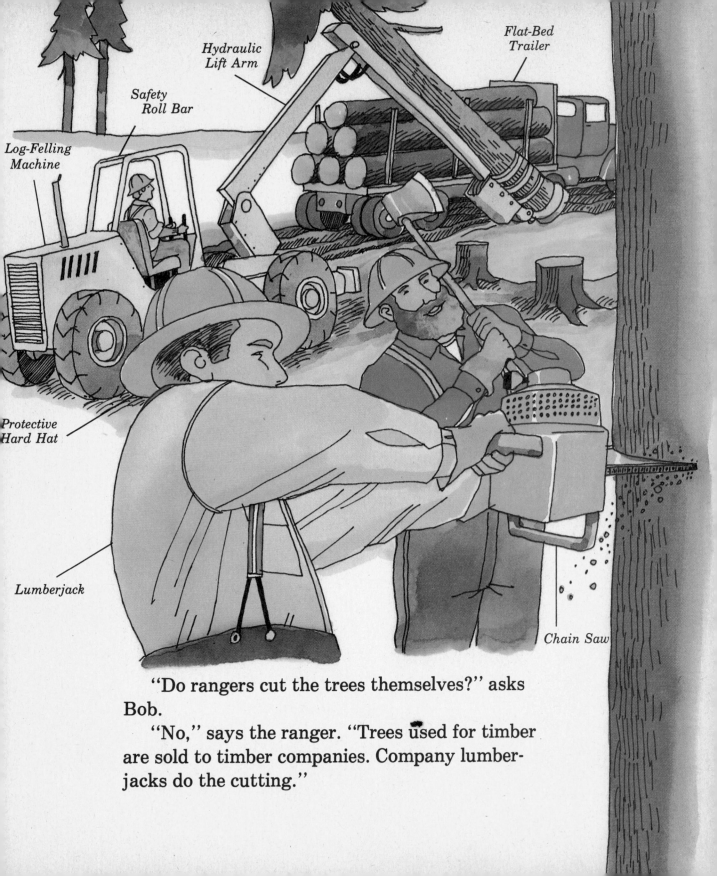

Hydraulic Lift Arm

Flat-Bed Trailer

Safety Roll Bar

Log-Felling Machine

Protective Hard Hat

Lumberjack

Chain Saw

"Do rangers cut the trees themselves?" asks Bob.

"No," says the ranger. "Trees used for timber are sold to timber companies. Company lumberjacks do the cutting."

Jim takes Bob on a ride through the forest. "Many rangers specialize in wildlife," says Jim. "They make sure wild animals have a good home in the forest. They plant trees that give the animals food and shelter."

Seat Belt

Four-Wheel Drive Jeep

Ear Tag

"Look," says Bob. "There's a mother bear
and her cubs."

"Each one is tagged and has a number," says
the head ranger. "Keeping track of forest animals
is part of the job, too!"

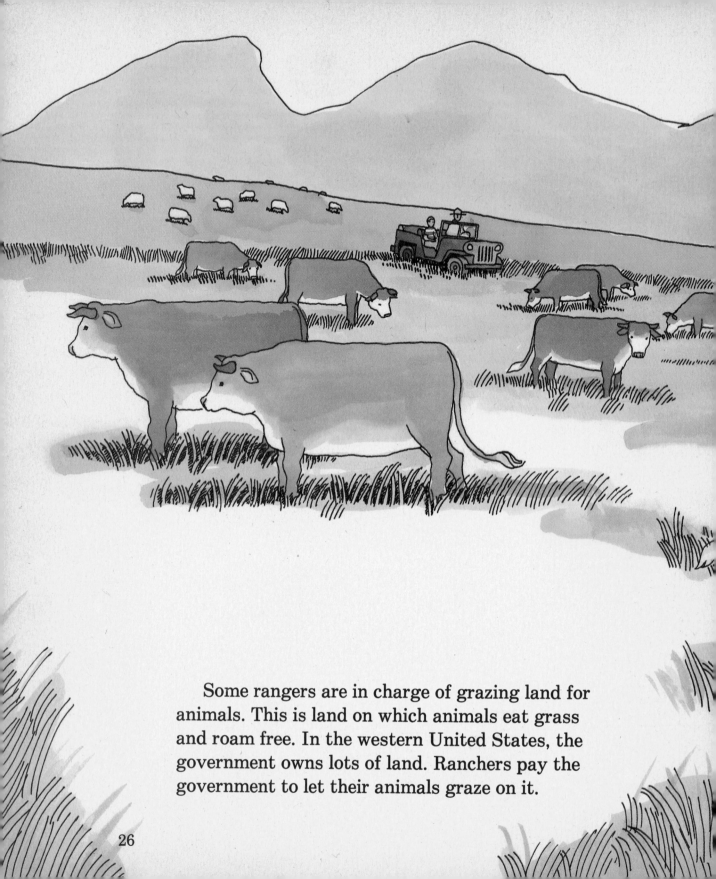

Some rangers are in charge of grazing land for animals. This is land on which animals eat grass and roam free. In the western United States, the government owns lots of land. Ranchers pay the government to let their animals graze on it.

Cattle and sheep graze on the land. Wild animals eat the grass, too. Rangers make sure there is enough food for all the animals. They also check the soil to make sure it is in good condition.

Spare Tire

Seat Belt

Brake Lights

"The most valuable resource in our forests is water," says Jim, pointing to a waterfall. "Rangers must pay attention to the water needs in their area. They use special instruments to measure snowfall and how much snow melts."

The melting snow tells the rangers how much water to expect on the ground. Water is important for growing things.

Weather Instruments Center
(Humidity, Air Pressure, Temperature)

Snow
Moisture
Gauge

Snow Depth
Gauges

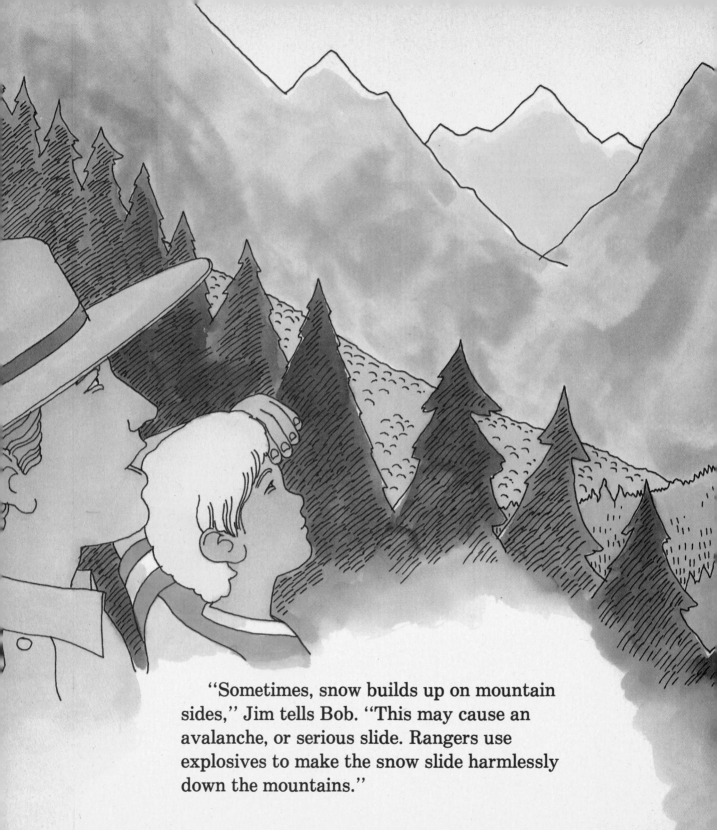

"Sometimes, snow builds up on mountain sides," Jim tells Bob. "This may cause an avalanche, or serious slide. Rangers use explosives to make the snow slide harmlessly down the mountains."

Sliding Snow   *Rangers*

BOOM! WHOOSH!
Jim and Bob watch some snow slide gently
from the mountain top.
   "The mountain is safe now," says Jim.
Bob sees two rangers ski away.

31

"Wow!" says Bob. "I had no idea that forest rangers do all those things!"

"Do you still want to be a ranger?" Jim asks with a smile.

"More than ever," answers Bob.

"Well," says Jim, putting his ranger's hat on top of Bob's head, "maybe someday you will."